Nearly Naked

By

Patrick O'Neill

Llumina
PRESS

Credits

Thanks to the following artists for their revealing and provocative contributions to *Nearly Naked*.

Cover: Oil on Canvas, by Grady O'Neill.

Water Color illustration for "Dude in the Tube," by Polly Barbacovi.

Illustrations for "Single Stream" and "Rise and Fall of the New Old," by Bill O'Neill.

ISBN: 978-1-62550-510-1

Contents

Preface

A key poem of my past that busted into the right chamber of my brain and demonstrated for the theme and poems of this book.

(From my book *Deciduous*):

Ooah- Coo- Coo- Coo

By Patrick O'Neill

I walk into the tavern, sit at the bar.
The residue of combat
with administrators and parents
over a book they want to pull
from my freshman comp class—
citing profanity, explicit sex scenes
as detriments to the students'

social development—is beating

against the inside of my head

like a huge pair of wings—

like an eagle that wants out—

that I'm trying to let out.

I order a beer, take a long drink,

and begin picking up on

what a young guy

a couple stools down—

baldy haircut—is telling

the bartender: His mom

made him go outside

to sheer his hair—he stretched

the extension cord to the edge

of the rock garden—left his hair

in a pile there. In the house,

his mom yelled at him

to get back outside, clean it up.

But as he headed back,

a mourning dove swooped down,

grabbed a tuft and flew away—

then another and another.
He spent the afternoon
watching the doves remove his hair.

I ask him why he cut his hair off.
He looks pensive for moments,
then says, Because my mom likes
it long—she says there's something
obscene about a naked head—
or a naked anything for that matter.
Rebellion turned benefactor,
he said. I'm really into birds.
I photograph them, count them,
feed them, draw them, and call them.
This is the first time
I've supplied them
with building material.
Then he floats refrains
of the dove's song by me—
ooah-coo-coo-coo.
The beating wings in my head
find an open window,

releasing the eagle,

and a childhood morning fills

a neglected neighborhood

with budding sunlight,

a cool breeze, and peace.

I think of the guy's gift

of hair and tell him

the doves are lucky his mom

thinks naked is obscene.

I buy him a beer and return

to my quickly fading

childhood early morning,

when a thought flaps

through the neighborhood:

It perches on a lower branch

of a birch tree and says:

Let's all undress

our thoughts, feelings—

share their stark nakedness

and watch a peaceful transformation

glide across the planet.

In that neighborhood,

as the morning sun blooms,

I watch a young boy—bare-ass

naked—summer haircut—

happy and free—run down

a path to the creek,

an *ooah-coo-coo-coo* chasing him.

And I feel the penetration

of the glaring revelation

that terrorizes dictators,

rallies censors—

and lines the nests of doves.

Prologue

Before you begin exploring the pages of my book, I'd like to introduce you to one of the narrators and his niece who both frequently pop up in my poems. (Excerpt from "Annihilator of Action: The Playground" [P. 41]):

My niece, daughter

of my sister, the botanist,

and a zoology major

at the University,

returns from a cruise

in the Caribbean she calls

a Meditation-Contemplation

Retreat. When I ask her

what that entails,

she hesitates then says,

"You know, taking your mind

off your work and other
stressful activities you have
to deal with." I ask, "Like school
and your involvement
with PETA and WSPA and other
animal organizations
where you help your animal friends
survive the onslaught
of human intervention
that critically abuses many animals—
wild as well as domestic—
and threatens
to wipe out entire species?"
She hangs her head and nods.

I say, "Watch out for Contemplation
and meditation. When you
employ them to heal and inspire,
they're good friends.
But they too often sneak
Aboard luxury liners

that move

from institution port to institution port—

loading up

with splurge, neglect,

and squander—that settle

in passive ports and puddles

of waste. *Action* that avoids

institution-bound luxury liners

aggressively rides alone

in currents and rapids

that rush by the institutions—

`streaming

into roiling pools of worth."

My niece says, "Sounds

brutal. Can I wear

a life jacket?"

I shake my head and say,

"No!" "Okay," she says.

"Will you toss me a life line

if I need it?" "No, I say.

"But if I can get ahold of one,

I'll send a porpoise
to the rescue." She laughs
and says. "Deal! Or maybe
if the weather's warm enough
a sea turtle so I can have
a smoother ride—relax and enjoy
dumping all the stress I have
to deal with."
"Maybe," I say, "I should send
a shark to keep you busy." She points
her tongue at me and says,
"You're acting like a little kid.
A porpoise will do nicely."
I stick out my naked, unabashed tongue
and give it an audience until my niece
strips off the costume of Pretend,
wags her tongue at me and says,
"Sharks will only keep
me busy avoiding their attacks. . . ."

Nearly Naked

From *Mother Goose Nursery* Rhymes:

Hey! diddle, diddle,

The cat and the fiddle,

The cow jumped over the moon;

The little dog laughed

To see such sport,

And the dish ran away with the spoon.

The Dish Runs After the Spoon

(A Nearly True Story)

Taking a break from a rough day

of fighting commanding

institutional restraints to get

to where I have to be

to accomplish what I

desperately feel I have

to accomplish, I listen

to my sister. the botanist,

read nursery rhymes

to her daughter

from *Mother Goose*.

My fear that I'm losing the battle

with Institutional restraint

gets tangled in the last verse

she reads: "Hey! diddle, diddle."

When I leave to return

to the battle front, a dish

running away with a spoon is

reverberating over and over

in the right chamber

of my mind. To better prepare

myself for the ensuing battle, I decide

to delay my attack and build

a vehicle to carry a dish

and a spoon

to the battle front

to reinforce my tiny regiment.

The Vehicle:

Quit and Defeat

Quit and Defeat are
like dishes fighting
over spoons. It's a matter
of taking control
of my spoons and what dishes
I scoop from. I can't let
the tempting tasty dishes
of assorted mind and body toxins
wearing uniform costumes
of health and wellbeing
that institutional chefs
prepare decide what spoon
it craves. What I spoon
into my being has to pass
my thorough examination
of the ingredients of what's
on the dishes before I decide.

3

It's a steep, grueling trek

to get my spoons

to the dishes

that hold the genuine

nutritious victuals.

After I manage

to strip Health

and Wellbeing disguises

off institutionally embellished

dishes of toxins, the challenge

grows more persistent

and difficult. If I fold,

Quit takes over and I

spoon from the tempting,

easily accessible dishes filled

with destructive toxins

and hollow calories. When I

fight the impending failure—

endure the pain, and give

my all to reach my goals—

even if Defeat stops me short

of the premier dishes—

I spoon nutrition and incentive

from dishes of my efforts.

Defeat can be a great chef.

Quit's a lousy one.

I return to the battle front;

and, in a tough fight,

I ride the dish-spoon vehicle

to victory. I get to where I

have to be and do what

I have to do. And I return

to my next battlefront

with renewed spirt and energy.

I'm still in the driver's seat

of the dish-spoon attack vehicle—

and we're stripping

and tossing disguises

off plates of poisoned

institutional bait

to beat all Billy Hell.

Beasts

After a tense, futile

negotiation meeting

with the College

Board of Trustees,

I'm sitting

at a coffee shop

with a friend

I've had since childhood,

who just recently became

my colleague as a member

of our English Department.

I ask her, "Remember

when we were in high school

we wrote support letters

for the students

in the Supreme Court

censorship case against

the Island Trees School Board?

(See end note.*)

She laughs and says, "The one

that got me the most

was the book they jerked

because of Swift's essay,

'A Modest Proposal,'

like the essay was

actually recommending

that the Irish slaughter,

cook, and eat

their children

to ward off famine!"

"At least they got

part of it," I say.

"Yeah. And here we go again."

"Scary," I say. "Who

would imagine

that nearly thirty years

later school boards would

still be playing the same games—

and winning some of them?

Censorship's durable, resilient."

"Like a cat," she says"—
"nine lives."

"No," I say. "They would have
expired long ago.
It's like a multitude
of armies
of combat-ready
maladjusted beasts
that multiply like rabbits.
All we can do is
keep fighting
to eliminate
as many as we can—
weaken their offense,
put them on defense."
"When do we walk?" she asks.

"About an hour," I say.

"Got your sign?" she asks.

"Yep," I say. "Scared?"

"Terrified," she says.

"Look," I say.
"You don't have tenure.
We're breaking a state law.
Sit this out; we'd understand."

"No. I'd lose something
more important
than my job: my integrity.
Let's go butcher,
cook, and eat
some beasts—yank some
of the tooth and claw
out of another
in a perennial series
of first-amendment assaults."

"And unlike Swift," I say,
"We'll keep

our reform operations

in their birthday suits—

clear, sharp, and literal."**

*In 1982 the Supreme Court decided a suit in favor
of five students who filed it against the Island Trees
School Board for banning a number of books
because they were "anti-American, anti-Christian,
anti-Semantic, and just plain filthy."

** And we did it!

My Grandma's Deck Hands

I guess I lost you
a few hundred muddy words
back," my grandma says.
I say, "You muddy-well have."
"Muddy" as a noun, verb,
adjective, adverb sails
on a vessel (as do
other words and phrases
she launches)
into my grandma's rhetoric
like a meddlesome prankster.
The word stowed away
on a ship from England
and hung around.
Some people, especially
those of English descent,
like Grandma, must like
the strong two-syllable punch
of the word. It's
a one-two effect—

like another of her vessel's

deck hands "bloody."

I enjoy the command

in vivid color the deck hands

bring to the vessels

she launches

to accentuate her points.

I return to the core

of my attempt

to clear the way

for my grandma to see

and appreciate the reasoning

justifying my stand

on a recent involvement

with a school administrator,

whose wife is a member

of my grandma's church.

Grandma claims I belittled

and embarrassed

both him and his wife

when I defied him

and ignored one

of his policies

that prohibited a newly

married gay couple

from speaking

at a well-attended,

student-sponsored

college event. My grandma's

demeanor tells me

I'm making progress.

In spite of her allegiance

to the church, she regularly

breaks out of the lockup

and thinks above, around,

and beyond it.

Her voice and face soften

as she begins to recognize

and accept the illegality

and unfairness of the policy.

She uses another phrase

from her army of deck hands.

It's a deck hand

that may have hitchhiked

from Scotland and stowed away

on that same ship

with "Muddy." She says,

"Well, you'd better *redd up*

your sensitivity,

and while you're at it,

redd off that table

of assorted rhetorical arsenals

you use to attack

people who can't help

who they are

or what they believe—

who can't tolerate

your bloody determined,

demanding liberalism that

has forged left since you

were a baby." I almost go

for launching a defense

but decide, What the hell!

She's *my* grandma.

And grandmas are hard nuts

and bolts to turn. Besides,

she's already nearly run
my bloody WD-40 vessels
out of ammunition.
And without the WD-40
I'm apt to snap one
of those nuts or bolts
that keep her tough
and independent enough
to bust out
of the church's bastilles
so she can be who,
deep down, she is
and she can redd up
her deck hands
to reveal her bloody gut-level
feelings and thoughts.

Academy? Emmy? Grammy? Tony?

I sit in a West-End Tavern

and listen to a couple men

down the bar, watching

kick boxing on TV, brag

about how tough their sons

are and reinforce their claims

with the graphic details

of blood and bruises

of their son's

recent trumpings—

and their reputation,

monetary, and opportunity

gains at the expense

of their victims' severe losses.

I was hoping to relax and give

the right chamber

of my brain a day off,

but the men's attitudes

and harsh revelations
of their sons' behavior call
him back to work. I pull
my writing pad out
of my paper holster
I always carry on my belt
and begin to scribble
the first draft of this poem:

Violence climbs into many costumes.
A seasoned actor, he repeatedly
grabs lead roles from Love.
He sparkles as he dances, sings,
dramatizes, orates in commanding
performances that portray
countries' love for their people
by sending them to war to pillage
and kill to increase the power
and wealth of controlling
minorities. Violence again shines
in his performances as men
who show their love

for their sons by—throughout

their sons' trips to puberty—

training them to win fights

at nearly any cost

and ruthlessly grab

what they can

from the victims.

These are only two

of many productions

in which Violence

plays commanding roles

as Love, captivating

huge international audiences.

Violence's sterling performances

demand the world

recognize him as one

of the foremost, talented

actors in the last

1500 or so millenniums.

It's painful, but I'm

in the process

of stripping him

of his costumes

of pretenses and taking

a closer look

at the circumstances

behind some of the scenes

of the most recent productions

he's starred in. I'm hoping

to find evidence

he's getting old, losing his touch,

collapsing, and ready

to strip off the costumes and retire.

So far he just flaunts

his acting awards,

laughs at me

and continues to kick ass.

The Stallion—the Uterus—the Myth

Fear lurks in Old Age;

Fear strikes me.

I play around with Analogy.

Uncertainty overwhelms

me. Fancy sells me

assorted synthetics.

Subconscious hoards

what I need back:

the warmth and blackness

and wetness of the womb crib—

the trauma of the big dump

into light and space and cold.

Consciousness corrals

and hobbles me

like a young quarter horse—

for my own good, he says.

He tries to explain away

the discipline: "They're saving

part of it for the exit:

Look at those heroes

of resurrection

who come back

to write books and revive

the talk shows with their stories

about dark tunnels

with glowing ends."

Consciousness doesn't

convince me, and I give him

trouble with the lead.

He holds and tethers.

He gilds me. I tug. He walks

me back to when I was

in my single digits.

I tug. He commands me

to stand. I can't. I pull and jerk,

but Consciousness stays

in command. Yet I sense a concern,

like he knows the years are fraying

the lead—gnawing at his control.

(He and the lead and I age together,

but I think I am strongest.)

I wait and, gilding like, grow old.

It is late. I call to the past.

Stallion-hood flickers.

I react with resurrected reflexes

and pull quickly

with stallion-like abandon.

Something lets loose

and I'm there: moving

from the warm, wet blackness

of the womb, busting

through membrane,

A force probes, pulls me—

toward the glow

at the end of the blackness. I

move through blood

and discharge and stench

until Cold and Light

blast me with a terrifying emptiness.

Then Consciousness harnesses me

and turns me back to the tunnel

with the glowing end.

I obediently cantor

toward the glow.

For a while. Then nothing.

Mess and Motion

A woman who babysat me
when I was in my single digits
used to say, *You clean up a mess*
and mess up a clean. Then you have
another mess. It keeps you in motion—
racing instead of moseying,
doing instead of malingering.
Motion is what keeps us alive.
Clean up a mess. Mess up a clean.

I've rarely met as snappy a piece
of philosophy since. I've ridden a lot
more years than the circumstances
of my life should have saddled up
for me—longer than I imagined. I'm still
on the track racing through the years,
flaying my messed-up cleans
and cleaned-up messes—
with my messed-up cleans leading
my cleaned-up messes by furlongs.

I calculate Cleans haven't a chance

to catch Messes—which I imagine

would mark the end of my racing.

But either way, soon Time

and Circumstance will run me

off the track—clean out

of the direction and motion

to ride a Clean or a Mess to victory

or even a respectable finish.

Recently, now that

I've galloped

into my double digits

rapidly nearing

my triple digits, the woman

who baby sat me

in my single digits

and inspired this poem

visits me. I share

this horse-racing analogy

with her. Giving me her

you-should-know-better look

and shaking her index finger

at me like she used to do

when she baby sat me

and I did or said something

she considered stupid, she says,

"You're old enough to know

that horse racing is

a firmly established mess:

a mistreatment

of the poor animals

who they whip and spur

and the people who abuse

themselves and others

who become addicted and take

essential money from their budgets—

from their families—to squander

on betting on the races.

Get off that race horse

and learn to stay in motion

by racing, walking, and trekking

on your own two bloody feet."

 I thank her for smacking me

with another snappy piece

of philosophy.

It turns up the volume

on what I need

to pay more attention to:

I'll never become experienced

or wise enough to dismiss

revelations of wisdom

that I accumulated

as a child. She lambasts me

with the painful

but realistic revelation

that racing I'll never

ride through

enough years

of exploration and discovery

to dismiss the theories

and revelations

of old and new babysitters

who are concerned enough

to give me refresher

feeder courses or offer

fresh innovative feeder courses

to chase me away

from debilitations
like Race Tracks.
My single-digit baby sitter
just knocked me
off my horse
and back on my own
rugged path
where—until Circumstances
permanently delete
my animation—
on my own two feet,
I'll trek wildernesses
of wild pristine Revelations
where in unpredictable,
intensive, and potentially
worthy motion—I'll mess up
my cleans and clean up my messes.

Amputations

Following are a few of the words of revelation and resolve I overheard as I sat at the bar at Tacconellis' Supper club. They boomed from a group of men at a table who just spilled out of some sort of brotherhood meeting from one of the banquet rooms. They all laughed and voiced their agreement at each other's words of wisdom that were riding in buggies of macho-crippled reasoning processes—dressed up in institutional garb to resemble sound convincing observations and conclusions. I shuddered. Listen:

Women are different
from men.
Yeah: They flaunt
tits and asses;
they have babies.
Take my sister Suzie.
She's one of them feminists
Who claims that's

as far as it goes.
Anyone knows
that if you cut off
a man's leg or arm
or pecker It's going
to affect his mind.
And I say, Look,
Kate, If one thing
about something's
different then it's
all different. But she
can't see that women
ain't the same caliber
as men and then
wonders why I keep
calling her
a flakey female.
Them bughouse women's all alike.

Visage

Our new College President
walks into my office
for the first time;
it's a get-acquainted meeting.
I'm honest; he listens
to mostly what he doesn't
want to hear. I notice
that he only takes his eyes
off my littered desk
to scrutinize my shaggy beard,
my summer Kromer
polka-dot railroad hat,
and worn Levis'. As he leaves,
I can tell he lugs away
a heavy impression.

At our first staff meeting,
he tells us he's going
to "step on some toes"—
then launches a spiel

on proper grooming, dress,
and good housekeeping.
He mentions neatly kept beards,
professional attire, tidy desks.

Later, in my office, I sit,
pondering my desk top:
books, pencils, pens, papers
of assorted sizes and purposes
all scattered among
three scatter-bound piles
of comp and lit papers;
 a coffee cup my work-study student
gave me with the adage:
SOUNDS LIKE BULLSHIT TO ME;
a dirty spoon and knife; a lamp
whose base features
figurines of Bambi,
his mom, and Thumper;
a few pieces of pop corn
and other crumbs
from previous lunches;

legal pads that showcase
scrawl, doodles, food stains;
a rock; a chunk of copper
from a Copper Country mine;
a coffee can for clips and things;
other miscellaneous matter.

I see a wilderness I inadvertently
put together—full of mysteries
of what was and what will be.
He saw a helter-skelter of rubble
mocking the civilized order
of institutional disciplines.

I sit pondering, feeling bad,
knowing what the poor guy
expects to find next time
he visits me. I'm wondering
if he has a right to expect it
when something lurking
in that wilderness rises
to its haunches, howls

at the Bambi lamp light.

Bambi's mother is bedded—

secure in the shelter

of *Great Short Works*

of Mark Twain,

the *MLA Handbook*,

a pile of paper towels,

other assorted things—

and the open-book lamp

back drop, featuring

the dialogue between

Bambi's mom and Thumper

that christens the fawn.

I look at Bambi's mom.

I feel good. I defended

her wilderness. I didn't

wrap it in a costume;

I left it bare/naked—

as Popeye would say:

'Tis what it 'tis. Now,

on his infrequent visits

to my office, the Dean

mostly looks
at the ceiling,
and Bambi's mom
raises her head
from her son, sleeping
at her side; she gives me
that special look that's
so securely locked in sincerity
that only animals can wear it—
the one that overflows
with gratitude and trust.

I stroke my shaggy beard,
tip my polka-dot hat.
Then I enter my wilderness
of mysteries of what was
and will be and trek
among the books papers,
and miscellaneous debris
of who I "yam."

Special Forces of the Warrior Naked

I stand outside

the study door

and overhear my Aunt June

scold Uncle Ray

for abandoning the church

and refusing to participate

in a movement to support

a clutch of right wingers

who were hell bent

to remove a few liberals

from the school board

who were defending

the freedom of students

to express their views

in the school paper.

Being careful not to be

too offensive and ignite

her wrath, he defends himself

with what impresses me

as being something

he's prepared for.

He says, "I don't have the time

for allegiances or alliances—

nor can I afford to lose

what parts of me

I've managed to salvage

during my long, rough odyssey

through years at war

with institutional forces

heavily armed

with mandates, rules, threats,

doctrines—blasting away

at my individualism—

the real Me—attempting

to convert Me

to a crippled conformist.

Luckily, I've been

strong enough to build

a defense that maintains

enough of the real Me

to trek pristine wildernesses

that allow me to explore

and use what I discover

to give what comes

from the Essence

of My Being that's

not contaminated

with the potent poisonous,

contagious Influences

of dictatorial Institutions."

My Aunt June laughs

her favorite laugh—

the one that dances

in sarcasm

and after the dance

before Uncle Ray can

respond, she storms

out the door, catches

me eavesdropping,

and launches

a loud scolding routine

that's almost scary—

promising me that I'll

suffer for it in the hereafter.

Just when she really

gets into it, Uncle Ray

saunters out the door

and calmly says to her,

 "And I forgot to mention

another important

crippling institutional alliance."

She stops yelling,

and he says "Marriage."

When she begins yelling

at him, he signals me

with a subtle wink

and a slight swing

of his head. I answer

with a curt nod

and hightail it

out of the house, carrying

revelations that have taken

the long rough

battle-ridden ride

with me to where I am now

and have stripped me

of the uniforms

of institutional conformity,

exposing me bare ass—

and—like Uncle Henry—

delivering the raw,

unembellished revelations

of what I think and what

(unfortunately) I am.

Thanks, Uncle Ray and Aunt June.

Annihilator of Action

(The Playground)

My niece, daughter
of my sister, the botanist,
and a zoology major
at the University,
returns from a cruise
in the Caribbean she calls
a Meditation-Contemplation
Retreat. When I ask her
what that entails,
she hesitates then says,
"You know, taking your mind
off your work and other
stressful activities you have
to deal with." I ask, "Like school
and your involvement
with PETA and WSPA and other
animal organizations
where you help your animal friends
survive the onslaught

of human intervention

that critically abuses many animals—

wild as well as domestic—

and threatens

to wipe out entire species?"

She hangs her head and nods.

I say, "Watch out for Contemplation

and meditation. When you

employ them to heal and inspire,

they're good friends.

But they too often sneak

aboard luxury liners

that move

from institution port

to institution port—

loading up

with splurge, neglect,

and squander—that settle

in passive ports and puddles

of waste. *Action* that avoids

institution-bound luxury liners

aggressively rides alone

in currents and rapids

that rush by the institutions—

`streaming

into roiling pools of worth."

My niece says, "Sounds

brutal. Can I wear

a life jacket?"

I shake my head and say,

"No!" "Okay," she says.

"Will you toss me a life line

if I need it?" "No, I say.

"But if I can get ahold of one,

I'll send a porpoise

to the rescue." She laughs

and says. "Deal! Or maybe

if the weather's warm enough

a sea turtle so I can have

a smoother ride—relax and enjoy

dumping all the stress I have

to deal with."

"Maybe, I say "I should send

a shark to keep you busy." She points

her tongue at me and says,

"You're acting like a little kid.

A porpoise will do nicely."

I stick out my naked, unabashed tongue

and give it an audience until my niece

strips off the costume of Pretend,

wags her tongue at me and says,

"Sharks will only keep

me busy avoiding their attacks;

sea turtles will allow me time

and give me incentive

to keep busy coming up

with ideas that we can

implement to keep the poor things

and other animals from becoming extinct."

I smile, nod, and say,

"I'll find two of them—

female and a male. That way

you can have a lively debate.

She nods and says, "Better find three—

two males and a female.

That'll even up the gender ratio.

Dude in the Tube

(For Polly Barbacovi)

(Water Color by Polly Barbacovi)

My girlfriend and I walk along
a Mediterranean resort beach
near Puerto Aventura
where her sister has a
condo

she's letting us use.
Suddenly she pokes me,
points, and says, *"There's*
an image of a classic
American
success and wellbeing
story
if there ever was one."
I watch a fat man in a bathing suit,
a floatation tube
around his waist, a large cigar
clamped in his mouth
that's jerking up and down,

like an impatient erection,

as he talks to a young girl

who's attached to his arm

and laughing at whatever he's

telling her that probably isn't

even funny. He's waddling

the girl across the beach

toward the beer garden.

I say, "Yeah, success and wellbeing

that translates to failure

and misbeing." She nods,

looks up at me, and asks, "Misbeing?"

"Overindulging and self-centeredness,"

I say. She asks, "Do you think

maybe you're headed

in that direction?" I pretend

to take the question seriously

and say, "Must be or I wouldn't be here."

"Don't be foolish" she says.

"Remember, I had to coax to get

you here." "What'd it take—

three words?" I ask. She pauses,

counts on her fingers,

and says, "Five. They were:

"Don't be such a dud." "Yeah," I say,

"but it was what your eyes

were screaming and threatening

that got me here." She reaches

over and jerks my polka-dot hat

off that I wear constantly.

The hat has been a camp ground

for people and places that have had

powerful emotional impacts

on me over the last thirty years.

It began with my Uncle Henry—

an old railroad man who wore

the railroad summer

Kromer polka-dot hat

year around. But that's a story

that demands and deserves

its own exclusive vehicle.

My girl waves the hat and says,

"You realize the only time I see

your hair is when we go to bed—

and that's only when I can get

my eyes to coax you to take it off."

I shrug; she reattaches the hat

to my head, and we follow

the guy in the tube

with the young girl attached

to his arm to the beer garden.

At the bar a bulging man

in a striped suit is passing out fliers.

My girl takes one, begins

reading it, then she waves it

at me and says, "You've got to listen

to this. There's a Vegas bar and grill

called The Heart Attack Grill

that lets people over 350 pounds

eat free. They serve things

like 8,000 calorie octuplet Bypass

burgers w/40 bacon slices;

½ pound Coronary Dogs.

And on their one-item vegan menu

is Salad: 100% leaf Tobacco—

no meat additives. Now they're

celebrating, as a hero, the first person

to die of a heart attack

at their bar and grill. Let's go

to Vegas and explore how people—"

she flicks my hat with her finger—

"who don't wear polka-dot hats live."

I say, "Close your god-damned eyes

or tell them to shut up." She says,

"Pay attention. You're not listening

to them. They're whispering."

"Sorry," I say, "make them whisper

a little louder." She closes then opens

her eyes. "How's that?" She asks.

I gaze into them. "Wow! They're

laughing." "That's funny," she says,

"I asked them to smile." I look again

and say, "Now they're giggling."

"They hardly ever giggle," she says.

Then engaging her mouth,

she giggles. "What's the giggle about?"

I ask. "You," she says. "Me?" "Yeah,

you can't translate the messages

of my eyes as well as you think you can."

"What were they whispering?" I ask.

"Take another look," she says.

I look into two seas of alluring,

provocative passion surrounded

by demanding facial animation.

She grabs my hand; and as she hurries

me to the privacy of the condo, I ask,

"Your eyes weren't passing out

Vegas fliers?" She laughs. "You think

I'd take a chance on ending up

with a dude in a tube instead

of a dud with a polka-dot hat attached

to his head?" Still, Doubt and Anxiety

plague me. It's like I feel she's playing

with me; I'm a toy windup mouse;

she's the cat. But at the condo,

on her sister's authentic

hand-knotted Tibetan Tiger Rug,

Ecstasy firmly clutches, constricts us,

exterminating pretending and deceit.

In a zip, the cat and toy mouse,

my Doubt and Anxiety perish when

in passion-packed spasms she,

breathlessly, repeatedly screams:

MY DUD. . . IN THE. . . POLKA-DOT. . . HAT. . . .

My. . . DUD. . . IN THE . . . POLKA-DOT. . . HAT.

Rise and Fall of the New Old

What we need, my niece, a zoology major

at the University, says, is a movement

that gets behind devolution and pushes

to beat Cheetah. Devolution? I ask.

Yeah, she says, we need to degenerate

some of the complexities of what we've

feasted on over the past million years or so.

That, I say, would be contrary to evolution.

Not at all, she says. Devolution is

on the same team as evolution.

We see it in the intriguing world

of animals all the time. Like? I ask.

Lampreys, she says. Parasitism

has caused them to degenerate

to jawlessness. Jawlessness? I ask.

She rolls her eyes at me and gives me

her mother's "You-stupid-fucker" look.

They've lost their jaws. Oh, I say.

We need more than ever, she says,

to practice devolution. Like how? I ask.

We need to change our mental

and physical diets. Take food, she says.

We need to regress to simple, primitive

eating habits that are healthy instead

of testing menus that are new

and more complex by using our children

as guinea pigs and watching them

become debilitated and dropping dead

of diabetic-related maladies

as young men and women. Just consider.

Our sense of smell has gone

to the scavengers through the centuries.

That's why we have to depend on dogs

to smell for us. Animals tell us the story.

Like we train dogs to smell for us,

we have to make more of an effort

to allow the animal world to see for us.

Before we slaughter them, look how

we deanimalize chickens, pigs, cattle

in torture chambers that masquerade

as farms—for food that, for the most part,

contributes toxins to our already

unhealthy diets. So, I say, the past

is clawing its way out of its grave

and we keep getting in its way. Yeah,

she says, we have to become more

like the animals and quit vacationing

in the past, get off our asses, and give

those scrappy warriors

who are fighting

to get back here

and fix what's wrong

a helping pair of claws

instead of a pair

that are digging a deeper pit

to bury the gifts

that could save us

from our reckless

disregard of our bodies, our minds,

and the planet. I admit, I say, there are

disadvantages to being what we call

the superior, reasoning beings. Yeah,

she says, thought that resides

in faulty reasoning processes

can be deadly. The animals live and die

by the wisdom of the universe

and we, she says, join forces

with the enemy—

accelerating debilitation

and killing by defying that wisdom.

I nod, look at my watch,

say, I've got to run.

Devolution is chasing me,

closing in on me—

and it's past my beer time.

My niece rolls her eyes

at me. They make think

that there's something

way too revealing

about the naked eye.

I close my eyes

so I can imagine

she doesn't notice

my eyes dim, rise,

then drop to the depths

of my eye sockets.

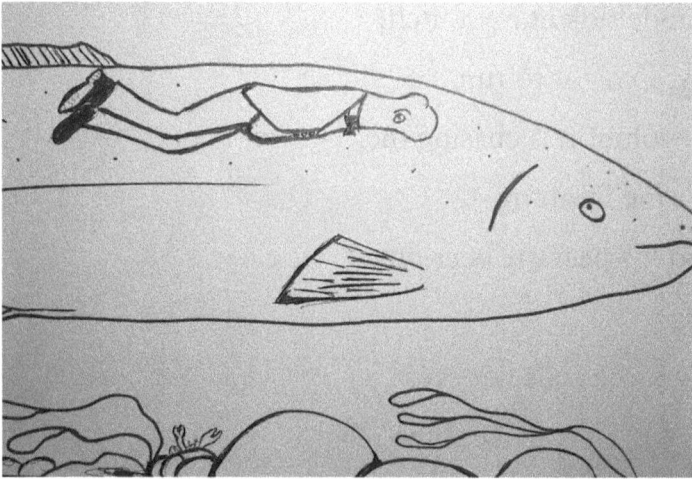

"Rise and Fall of the New Old"

Single Stream

I'm in the kitchen
of my friend Megan
replacing leaking drain pipes
under her sink. "Friends"
is a relationship I've
desperately been attempting
to pump intimacy
into and convert to "Lovers"
(in a sincere sense of the word).
I'm beginning to feel
my Desperation is
beating up on my Attempt.
Megan is a philosophy instructor
at the local college
and maybe connects
to some things too philosophically—
negating the philosophy.
I know that doesn't make
a lot of sense but neither
do most of the paradoxes

that clutter my thought processes
(like that one I just used).

Returning from a recycling run,
Megan bangs
through the kitchen door
and says, "WOW!
What a piece
of Limburger! I can throw
cardboard, newspapers,
cans, glass, plastic bottles,
and jars —almost anything
except plastic bags and garbage
in the same recycling bin." "That,"
I say, "is what they call
single-stream recycling."
She says, "They ought
to figure out how
to single-stream more things
in this complex departmental world.
We hide too many things
in separate, private departments

where we can't see them—

blinding us

to the processing activity

then deal with the results

like we know what's been going on."

"Like what?" I ask.

"Like living," she says—

"like I eat my meals. I put everything

on one plate and dump it

in one recycle bin." "What bin you using?"

I ask. "My fucking stomach," she says.

"My stomach runs it through tributaries

where it goes about doing

what it does before the tributaries

single-stream it to the toilet.

The toilet single-streams it

to ditches and sewers where it goes

through the same process.

Simple science," she says.

I say, "Maybe too simple

for the world to comprehend."

We look at each other and nod

sad concession. I get up

to leave. She asks, "Where you

off to?" "Hungry," I say. "I'm going

to throw some veggies,

peanuts, fruit, vinegar,

and almonds

in a bowl where everything

that's involved is

visible and enjoy

some single-stream recycling."

She says, "Nothing better or greener

than sitting down and dinning

with a renowned recycling bin."

I say, "Thanks for the lesson

in unadulterated,

naked revelations."

"Come along," I say,

"and we'll do a duet

of single streaming."

"Naked?" She asks.

The abruptness startles me.

I manage to nod and let out

an overly enthusiastic: "SURE."

"Only," she says,

"if you let me bring

my own food.

I'm not a fan of nuts."

I nod, grab her arm,

hurry her out the door.

When she begins

to resist, I say,

"We'll stop at Super One

and get you something to eat

besides nuts." She stops me,

pulls my head down

and with her lips

on my ear

and her tongue

caressing it whispers,

"No, this is

about single streaming

something more important

than food.

Nuts will do fine as bystanders."

We wake up late
that night
in each other's arms.
Neither one of us
remembers if we ate supper.
So we top off our first
real intimacy commitment
at my kitchen table,
holding hands and sharing
a jar of dry-roasted,
no-salt peanuts.
Later I toss the empty jar
in the paper shopping bag
she set up for me to recycle.
When we say good-bye,
she invites me
to single stream
at her place.
Before she
shuts the door,
she deposits a

peanut paradox

that I'll play with

off and on—while I impatiently wait

for our next single-streaming date:

She yells:

"DON'T FORGET THE-DRY-ROASTED

PEANUTS!"

"Single Stream"

Pain-Packed

I did something today
I felt good about. I dug
two wild horseradish roots,
and I hand-grated
horseradish.
The fumes stung
my sinuses,
watered my eyes.
The grating cramped
my arm, shaved skin
off my finger.
The experience
flushed, cleared
channels—alerted me
to the therapy of pain.
Things like horseradish
remind me that Pain—
if you let her/him—
can be a friend, doctor,
counselor, teacher.

So I tapped the pain.

I packed cups

of it in jars

with the horseradish

and raw vinegar,

integrating the pain,

horseradish, vinegar

(and its "mother")—

no intruding ingredients

(except for a little

blood and skin).

The experience

or the horseradish

won't do much

for me physically—

too late for that—

but it pumped

powerful juice

into the pistol

of my psyche.

It's enabled me

to disrobe and trash

Institutional fabrics

designed to blot out

or distort

raw revelations

of the good and the bad—

the lifeblood

of Truth and Beauty.

I learned long ago

that my endeavors

that require lots of time

and physical and mental exertion

and that focus on sacrifices

for the well-being of others

are as painful as All Billy Hell—

and the only endeavors

that make me feel good

about who I am

and that inspire me

to keep being what I am

and doing what I do.

Pain and I are

inseparable friends—

—and I couldn't

live without her/him—

even if at times

I have to resort

to packing her/him in a jar

of pickled horseradish.

Chefs

Love and Hate employ

Memory to cook up stories

about each other.

They serve them

in establishments

of grandiose décor,

high-toned waiters,

fancy tables,

too many plates,

and too much

silverware. It works

so well they have

involved couples

over-indulging

on cuisines that clash

like cymbals—both dishes

steaming with lies.

Lies are a delicacy

that entertain

and vitalize lovers.

Lies are the filet mignon,

lobster, prime rib—

the Riesling, Chardonnay—

of their dining. Love and Memory

are the esteemed restaurateurs.

A Solution

If you must dine

on your past out

of the plates, bowls, cups

of what others have prepared

for you, scrutinize the contents

for garnishes, additives, exterior décor—

any fancy outfits of deceit.

If you find any,

discard EVERYTHING immediately.

Ingest the revelations

of your past out

of your own plates, bowls, cups—

the love, the hate. Then let

the revelations guide you

to where you must go,

what you must avoid,

what you must embrace

to be what you must be:

The Nourishing, Naked YOU.

Bonappetit*

*My feeble attempt at irony to reinforce the narrator's classifying this kind of pretention as *poison.*

Synopsis of a Melodrama

The entire Play came to me in a long well-
produced, acted, and staged nightmare:

My Dream

In brief,
Greed and Vanity—
on patrol, bearing
state-of-the-arts weapons—
march on stage right.
They discover Natural Beauty
(center stage),
unarmed, in the company
of harmless, defenseless things.
Greed and Vanity
activate their weapons,
drive Natural Beauty
 to the Quicksand
of False Standards.

She screams for her lover.
Truth enters stage left,
runs to Natural Beauty.
She embraces him, clings to him,
inadvertently carrying him
to her own obscure grave.

When I awake and am able to finally recover from the impact of the nightmare, I begin to heal and to regard my recent loss realistically instead of melodramatically. Soon I find myself singing to myself the only verse I can recall that an old man used to sing repeatedly in a bar that I frequented when I was a freshman in college and, like me, had recently suffered the loss of a loved one to another man.

A friend caught me singing my verse a little too loudly to myself and the next day handed me a version of the entire song I hadn't asked for. She was like that—doing things for people that surprise them with usually what they don't want or need.

But I read the song and discovered that the old
man had modified the verse some. It's his version
that keeps me singing:

> Railroad, Steamboat, River and Canal
> Here's to the sucker who stole my gal
> Gone, Gone, Gone
> And I bid her my last farewell.

I find the verse reassuring.
It seems to resonate
of Realism that's tempting for me
to ignore. Realism has
multiple dimensions—many
of which are conflicting. I've learned
to focus more on keeping
culprits like Greed and Vanity
from distorting Reality
by obscuring key revelations
that conflict with what's most apt
to appease or— depending
on my temperament at the time—to anger.

For your scrutiny, I'm concluding

my poem with the version

of the entire song

my friend found for me,

whose short, modified verse

had such a lasting impact on me:

The Song:

Railroad, steamboat, river and canal

Yonder comes a sucker, and he's got my gal

And she's gone, gone, gone

And she's gone, gone, gone…

Railroad, steamboat, river and canal

Yonder comes a sucker, and he's got my gal

And she's gone, gone, gone

And she's gone, gone, gone

And I'll bid her my last farewell

I fell in love with a pretty little thing

I thought that wedding bells would ring

She was as sweet as sweet could be

'Till I found out what she did to me

Railroad, steamboat, river and canal

Yonder comes a sucker, and he's got my gal

And she's gone, gone, gone

And she's gone, gone, gone

And I'll bid her my last farewell

I asked her mother to let her go

She whispered, mother, please tell him no

Though he may think that I am true

There're plenty more who think so too

Railroad, steamboat, river and canal

Yonder comes a sucker, and he's got my gal

And she's gone, gone, gone

And she's gone, gone, gone

And I'll bid her my last farewell

Now I won't cry my life away

Some other sucker will have to pay

And when he finds that she is gone

I guess I'll hear him sing this song

Railroad, steamboat, river and canal

Yonder comes a sucker, and he's got my gal

And she's gone, gone, gone

And she's gone, gone, gone

And I'll bid her my last farewell.

The Ambiguous, Magic Metaphor

When my niece

accuses me

of being cheerful during

my late-afternoon beer break

and asks why I can't

be that way

all day long, I say,

"The cheer doesn't fit.

The cheer I've tried on

isn't the right color or size.

Sometimes I squeeze

into a beige gratitude

or contentment—but never Cheer.

Besides, it's out

of my budget range.

I tell her I quit shopping

for it. I make small parts

of my life reasonably tolerable

by running myself

through long, painful processes

of doing things

I don't like to do

(writing, teaching, running, etc.)—

then the reprieves

work like pain killers.

Guilt and Doing usually

fight to a draw,

belt each other listless—

so, by late afternoon, I

can have beers and celebrate

not experiencing

hard-core pain

until early morning.

Sometimes during reprieves,

my mind opens a chamber

and lets a particularly scrappy poem

bust in, fight its way

past the beers,

flatten my resistance, and knock

the living ingredients out

of reprieve. "You,"

I tell her, "caught me

with the beer swinging

like an angry Rocky Marciano,

behind in late rounds—

keeping Doing and Guilt

in the ring—tired, clinching—

and Reprieve on his feet."

"Why," my niece asks,

"don't you knock

the living ingredients

out of your metaphorical gobbledygook,

quit hiding behind boxers,

painkillers, and wardrobes—

and come to a reasonable facsimile

of a few of simple words

that carry the crux

of your intention?"

"Nicely put," I say.

"Hang on! The display

of cheer doesn't normally

have anything to do

with cheer.
It's either an attempt
to impress others or
to rationalize our behavior.
My recent display
was my psyche's attempt
to camouflage
my extreme discontent
with my lack of initiative,
inspiration, and productive action.
My niece says, "Wow!
That means when you're cheerful,
you're miserable
and when you're miserable
you're cheerful."
I nod and say,
"Metaphorically it does.
But your metaphor staggers
and wanders some.
You ought to add
a nutritious ingredient or so
to it to straighten it out."

"I would," she says.

But I'll leave that up to you.

You're the premier chef."

Simultaneously we both say,

"METAPHORICALLY!"

Guitars and Ukuleles

My "spanking new" wife
(A trite cliché that seems
to give more flavor
to the nature
of such relationships) is upset
because I didn't show up
for her Mother's
Easter dinner party.
I'm trying to explain to her
that it was an accident—
that it wasn't intentional;
I forgot it was Easter.

While she's screaming at me
that it's impossible to forget
such an important holiday,
I'm feeling a bit guilty
because missing the dinner party
is a huge boon to me.
I can't sit through gatherings

like meetings, conferences,

celebrations, parties, etc.

without feeling I'm losing

control and fighting temptations

to become destructive

and violent—even imagining

borderline homicide.

Although I'm certain

I'll never be

a threat to anyone,

when I make it through

one of the atrocious

spectacles, I feel certain

it's taken months,

years, even decades

off my life.

My "spanking new" wife

in a more civil tone

suddenly

(instead of screaming)

yells at me

that I'm a master

at pretending

to forget things

that I don't want anything

to do with and getting away

with it. Then she lectures me

on how it embarrasses her.

I try to explain

that I don't pretend not to

forget things. I confess

I sometimes I make an effort

not to notice things—

and it works. I say, "I did

remember it was almost Easter

on Thursday for a little while

because it meant I wouldn't have

classes on Friday and Saturday.

I remembered it for probably

a few hours after I got

your e-mail on Saturday.

Then I forgot about it

until about an hour ago

today, Easter,

and remembered only

because the teachers

who usually come to school

to work on Sunday mornings

weren't there.

That sent me back

to your e-mail and got me going.

Now I'll probably remember it

for the rest of the day

because the routine

will remain altered.

I'll have to enjoy

an Easter snack

in the kitchen—

stuff like that. I realize

my memory lapses

are likely due

to dead brain cells

from my boxing years,

or cells that weren't there

in the first place

that should have been.

But my mind has always

behaved this way—

as well as I can remember."

She softens a little,

smiles, and says,

"What a defense

for ignoring Easter!

It almost worked."

I say, "Remember just before

we married I mistook

your guitar for the ukulele

in the recording

of the recital you were making

me listen to?"

She laughs, says,

"I was infuriated.

Anyone should be able

to tell the difference between

a guitar and ukulele."

I say, "I've been fighting despair

that hangs around

with creative inactivity—

feeling guilty

about my feeble attempts

to produce something

strong enough

to feel good about.

Your Forgiveness

propels me to act;

it sends me soaring.

Resurrection!

What a time of the year

for the revelation!

I'm a believer.

Your Forgiveness

really motivates me—

because it's all you--no one else.

It's what I crave. I'm resurrected

and giving it "All Billy Hell"

thanks to you. I still and always will

have trouble distinguishing

between the strums

of guitars and ukuleles."

She laughs, says, "And Easter

and Christmas—

and The Opening Day

of Trout Season." She begins

to undress as we head

for the bedroom where

we help each other

undress and revel

in the crescendo

and climaxes

of our own special

Easter Resurrection—

Amid a mix

of plucks and pauses

that I construe to be playful

alert squawks riding

the twin strums

of guitars and ukuleles.

Spangles

(*For the Firefly Kids of Arlene Schneller's Creative
Incentive Class, Who Assigned the Poem—and Lifted,
Moved Me with Compelling Charges of Creative Energy*)

*My niece, a zoology major at the University,
flits into my office waving one of those jars
that seals with a wire clamp. She says,*
A fruit jar full of lampgridae, *like she expects me
to know what she's talking about. I don't;
I wait. Accepting my silence as a question—
using the tone and expressions many adults use
to chide a child for not having the right answer
to a trivial question—she says,* They're fireflies.

I nod and point at her fruit jar that I notice

has a modified top to admit air. I ask,

How long can they live in there?

Two, three days. I shanghaied them last night;

I'll free them tomorrow. It's like I'm taking them

on a travel tour. Tomorrow night they can

fly and flash the adventure to their friends

and families. They're delicate animals;

you have to be careful when you catch

and release them. How do you catch them?

I ask. Butterfly net. Removing them from the net

and putting them in the jar is tricky. You have

to take your time and be gentle. *I nod.* By the way,

I say, When I was a kid, we called—*I point*

at the jar—those lightening jars because

they sealed so quickly—and those creatures inside

lightening bugs. Okay, *she says,* so I have

a lightning jar of lightning bugs. That's better,

I say. When you go after fruit flies, you can call it

a fruit jar. And I can guess the mission

of the lightning jar of lightning bugs. Guess,

she says. You haven't paid your electric bill again

and the power company shut off your lights.

She doesn't smile. She says, Get serious.

They're for my class. You're taking a firefly class? *I*

ask.

She says, Of course not; it's for my entomology class.

Then—like I don't know what "entomology" means—

she says, Bug class. *I nod. She puts the jar on my desk,*

points at it, says, They're on their way out. Way out?

I ask. She nods, says, Like the Giant Panda,

Ivory-Billed Woodpecker, and Leather-Back Turtle,

they're high on the endangered species list.

If we don't do something soon, they'll be gone—

like the Baiji River Dolphin, Javan Tiger,

and Passenger Pigeon. What or who is spearheading

this firefly Holocaust? As usual, *she says,* humans are

in command. How, *I*
ask? Primarily light, *she*
says.

I give her a blank look. She
says, Light pollution.

Light pollution? *I ask.*

There's too much light
on this planet, and it's doing a lot of damage.
Darkness is as important to life as light is.
We've created an over balance of light.
Think about this: In large cities like Chicago
and New York, some adults who never
have left the cities have never seen
the constellations—never seen the Milky Way.
City lighting has extinguished them. What
about the fireflies? *I ask*. Excessive light
is our weapon of mass destruction.
They need darkness to communicate.
They flash for mates and to protect
themselves from predators.

Without darkness
they can't reproduce. If
chemical pollution
doesn't extinguish them,
light will.
What's anyone doing about this?
Attempting to preserve dark skies—
putting out some of the lights. As individuals,

we can simply make sure we don't leave

yard lights on unless we need them.

Many people burn them all night long. This

is all interesting and important, *I say*. But, you're

chasing away the mystery and invention that's

the essence of my relationship with fireflies.

Since I first discovered them when I was a kid,

I've come to know fireflies as miniature wizards,

beaming rays of light and rays of dark—daring me

to enter the prevailing darkness, confront the light,

and explore its mysterious wildernesses that reveal

the fireflies' secrets. The secrets frighten

and exhilarate me—inspiring me to pursue long,

difficult processes of invention and application.

Listen: Your lightning jar of lightning bugs

has expanded and magnified a recent experience

that flew out of nowhere and slammed me.

For the first time, last week, I visited a class

of the Creative Programs for Kids Series

that I fund through my book sales and ticket

and art sales from readings and books signings.

The class's reaction was overwhelming.

I walked out reeling from the impact

of the inspiration, energy, wonderment,

and creative motivation and determination.

Like the fireflies, the kids flashed and beamed

their inspiration, energy at me in the dark

and the light of

revelation. It

reinforced

my conviction that

wisdom doesn't come

from people wearing

neon-like, institutionally

acquired, important-sounding titles

like "professor," "sage," "scholar," "guru."

It comes in the dark and light of firefly flashes

from animals, plants, things, and—

most powerfully—from children. *As an afterthought, I*

say to my niece, I'll bet those people from New York

who've never seen the Milky Way have never seen

fireflies. She nods. Maybe on T.V. or a computer

or—if they're one

of the few of their generation who still reads—

in a book. And, *I add,* those sources or any other source

can't deliver the realism that generates wisdom like turning

the pages of a real night sky filled with the conversation

and calls of real fireflies. In firefly flashes, wisdom,

the child of unshackled sources, bellows charged clouds

of curiosity, doubt, exploration, discovery, creativity—

all alive with the power and will to recharge

dormant minds and bodies. If we stay alert, we

often discover wisdom in tiny, unlikely vessels:

like the figment-spangled thoughts

and pristine actions of young children.

My niece, who always craves the last say, adds,

And in the spangled, pristine revelations

of the mysterious, dynamic spellbinders—fireflies.

She grabs her lightning jar of lightning bugs,

jumps up from her chair, flits for the open door,

beats her arms like wings, and toe dances—

an attempt to impersonate a firefly. Then,

to add more spangle to her last say,

from the dimness of the hall, she points

at the fireflies and yells, THESE GUYS
WANT ME TO REMIND YOU TO MAKE SURE
THAT TONIGHT YOU TURN OFF YOUR
YARD LIGHT.

www.ingramcontent.com/pod-product-compliance
Lightning Source LLC
Chambersburg PA
CBHW061749020426
42331CB00006B/1402